Includes Five
SAT
Words to Know
MEETS STATE AND NATIONAL STANDARDS
China
IT'S YOUR WORLD
LIVE
WORK
PLAY
LEARN
Where Do You Want to Go?
A Great Wall Runs Through It!
Hey! It's the Great wall of China! Do you want to go?
TIME ZONE • CULTURE • CUSToMS • CLOTHING • HISTORY
FOOD • CULTURE • CUSToMS • CLOTHING • HISTORY • LANDMARKS
By Carole Marsh

Live • Work • Play • Learn

GALLOPADE INTERNATIONAL

Gallopade International is introducing SAT words that kids need to know in our books. The SAT words in this book have a gray box around them. Students can look up the definitions and increase their vocabulary. Happy Learning!

Gallopade is proud to be a member and supporter of these educational organizations and associations:

Association for the Study of African American Life and History
National Alliance of Black School Educators
American Booksellers Association
American Library Association
International Reading Association
National Association for Gifted Children
The National School Supply and Equipment Association
The National Council for the Social Studies
Museum Store Association
Association of Partners for Public Lands
Association of Booksellers for Children

At the time of publication, all websites referenced in this document were valid. However, due to the changing nature of the Internet, some addresses may change or the content become less relevant.

It's Your World Books

Africa: A Safari Through Its Amazing Nations!

Australia: The Land Down Under for Mates of All Ages!

Canada: The Maple Leaf Melting Pot Country!

China: A Great Wall Runs Thru It!

Egypt: An Ancient Land of Lore; a Modern Land of Oil and More!

France: The Ooh-La-La Country Everyone Loves!

Germany: The Country of Fairytale Castles and Cutting Edge Science!

Greece: A Volcanic Land of Ancient Olympic Origins!

India: Land of Six Senses and Intriguing Mystery!

Italy: The Country of Amazing Fountains and Awesome Arts!

Japan: An Island Country of Endless Intrigue!

Mexico: A Colorful Land of Exotic Culture!

Middle East: Ancient Countries of Current Events Headlines!

Russia: The Great Bear and Its Dramatic History!

South America: A Continent of Countries of Amazing Proportions!

United Kingdom: The Country of Ships, Sealing Wax, Cabbages, and Kings!

Other Carole Marsh Related Titles:

The Mystery on the Great Wall of China

Chinese for Kids

Table of Contents

A Letter from the Author

From the desk of
CAROLE MARSH

Hey kids,

It's your world! It really, really is!
Of course, you already know that, don't you?
You surf the 'net, listen to satellite radio, watch television shows and movies set all around the
globe—kids today are much more "worldly" than in the past, and that's a good thing!

Now's a great time to learn something about another country—such as China. Why? Because one
day, you might actually visit there (if you have not already!). You might go to school there—many
colleges have ties with international schools around the globe. You might even go on to work in a
foreign country!

Many companies have positions in other countries. Companies are "going global" as fast as they
can. They have branch offices, manufacturing plants, and customer service centers scattered
around the globe!

So, ready or not: YOU are a Citizen of the World! And you'll want to be a good one.
How do you do that? You'll find out everything you can about that country, how it's the same,
and how it's different from your own country. What language is spoken there? What customs
do the people observe? What foods do they enjoy? What do they
do for fun? What has happened in this part of the world,
and what is happening there now? It's fun ... and the more you
learn, the more you will enjoy whatever global opportunity comes
your way!

This book is a good place to start your learning journey—
so take advantage of the world—IT'S YOUR WORLD,
after all ... and guess what? It's a BIG world,
after all!

Happy traveling and learning,

Carole Marsh
Always with passport in hand!

Why Should We Care About China?

More than one billion people live in China. That's about one-fifth of all the people in the world. Although it is the fourth largest country, China is very crowded. That's because 90 percent of the people live on 15 percent of the land. Crops cannot be grown on most of the land in China! Growing crops is important for a country with so many people to feed.

For 3,000 years, outside influences did not change the traditional values of the Chinese people. Except in the large cities, people still live their lives in much the same way as their ancestors did. Chinese art forms and music are produced in much the same way as they were long ago.

Today, China is becoming a world superpower. The people of China struggle to balance their traditions with new ideas of the modern world. The Chinese people and their leaders are working hard to build a secure and prosperous nation.

One day, you might visit China to see the Beijing opera, study the "Three Perfections," live in an apartment in Shanghai, play soccer, or work for a Chinese company. It could happen!

Write home about it!
What will your postcard from China say?

Top Fast China Facts!

Important facts to remember about the country of China:

- China is officially called the People's Republic of China.
- China is a communist republic.
- The head of government in China is the Premier.
- Effective power is exercised by leaders of the Chinese Communist Party.
- The capital of China is Beijing.
- The currency used is the *yuan*.
- The official language is Mandarin Chinese.
- China is the oldest continuous civilization—3,000 years and counting!
- China has more people than any other nation in the world.
- China's largest city is Shanghai with 13 million people.
- The highest point on earth, Qomolangma (Mt. Everest) is on the China-Nepal border.

Now, you figure out the rest!

1. This is the Chinese ____ ____ ____ ____.

2. This is the national ____ ____ ____ ____ ____ ____ of China.

3. "March of the Volunteers" is the national ____ ____ ____ ____ ____ ____.

4. The ____ ____ ____ ____ ____ ____ ____ ____ name of China is the People's Republic of China.

5. The __ __ __ __ __ __ __ __ __ __of China is more than one billion people.

6. The Chinese call their country the ____ ____ ____ ____ ____ ____

____ ____ ____ ____ ____ ____ ____.

Where in the World Is China?

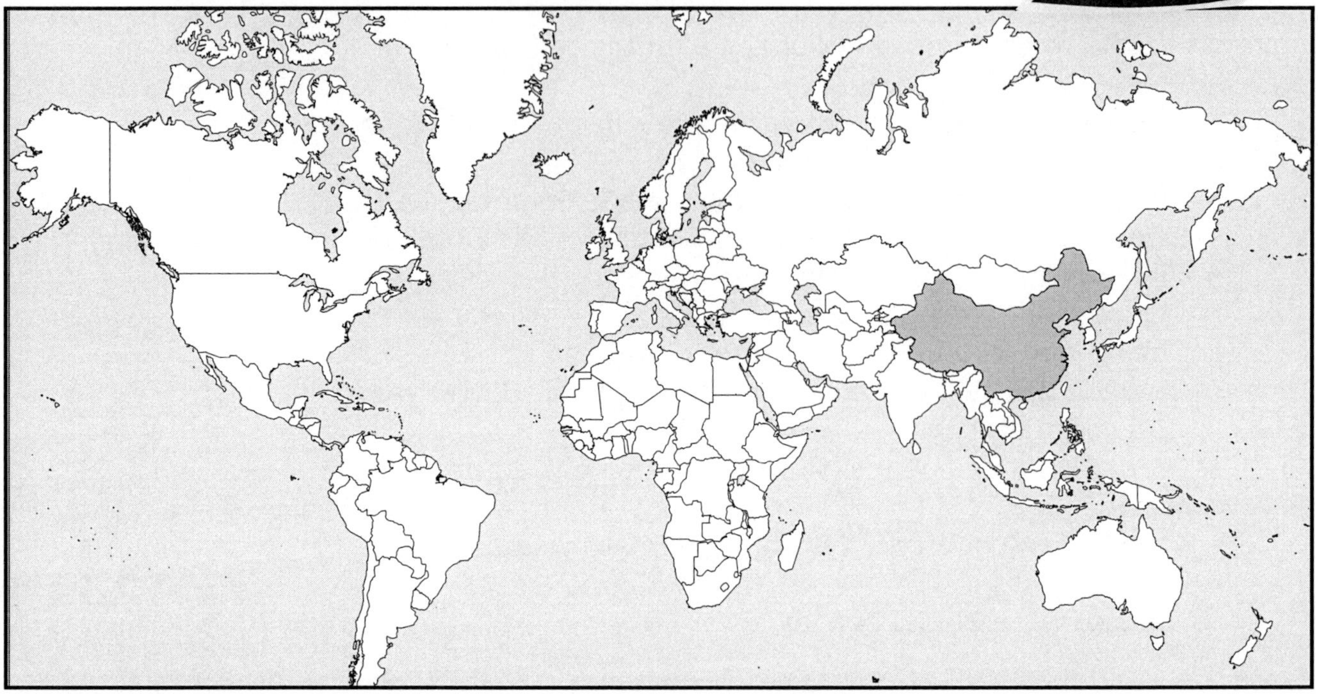

- China is the fourth-largest nation in the world.
- The 2008 Summer Olympic Games took place in Beijing, China's capital city.
- China is home to the world's tallest peak, Mount Everest, which is also located in the nation of Nepal.
- Some of China's neighbors are Mongolia, North Korea, Vietnam, Nepal, Pakistan, India, and Russia.
- The Great Wall of China is about 6,700 km (4,163 miles) long and is more than 2,000 years old!
- You can travel throughout this huge country and stay in the same time zone the whole time!
- The Chang (Yangtze) River is the third-longest river in the world.
- The Gobi Desert is the world's second largest desert.

Do You Know?

1. Ninety-five percent of the population is concentrated in the
   a. Eastern Region b. Western Region c. Northern Region

2. Only about twelve percent of China consists of
   a. mountains b. desert c. plains

Ancient China

Dynasties ruled China for more than 4,000 years! What is a dynasty? It is a series of rulers who belong to the same family.

The first Chinese emperor was Qin Shi Huangdi. Leadership in dynasties passed from father to son or to another male member of the family. Dynasties ended when someone from another family defeated the current ruler. Historians believe that there were about 13 dynasties, with the last one ending in 1912.

The last dynasty was the Qing. Although it ruled for almost 300 years, it was not as powerful as other dynasties. Foreign countries occupied parts of China. The Chinese people were unhappy with the government. The Chinese people called for revolution and defeated the last emperor of China in 1912.

Crosswords!

Use your new knowledge to fill in the crossword puzzle.

Across

2 Dynasties ruled China for over _______________ years. (2 words)

5 _______________ countries occupied parts of China during the Qing dynasty.

6 Leadership in dynasties passed to ____________ family members.

Down

1 The leader of a dynasty was the ________________.

3 Qin Shi _______________ was the first emperor.

4 Until 1912, China was ruled by _________________.

The Amazing History of China!

Dr. Sun Yatsen became the first president of the new Republic of China. China began as a land ruled by emperors. When the last dynasty was defeated, the new Republic of China was born. China would be a democracy governed by its people! Dr. Sun Yatsen was China's first President, but he resigned after only 2 months. He left the people of China in the hands of military leader Chiang Kai-shek.

Chiang Kai-shek

The Chinese people suffered greatly under Chiang Kai-shek. Five million people starved and 400,000 peasants sold themselves into slavery. At the same time, communists were gaining political power in China. Communists believe everything should be equal for people. In communist governments, people aren't allowed to own anything. Everyone must work for the good of the country. The government gives the people food, a job, and a place to live.

Chiang Kai-shek decided to fight the communists. After four years of fighting, he was forced to retreat to the island of Taiwan. China became a communist country ruled by Chairman Mao Zedong. He began a Cultural Revolution to erase all signs of China's past. Street and store signs with names of past Chinese rulers were removed. Government police, the Red Guards, took all property and possessions. Anyone who opposed his new policy was killed.

Chairman Mao died in 1976. China is still a communist country, but it is working to modernize. By growing economically, it hopes to improve the way its people live.

Timeline!
Number these events in the order they took place, first to last.

______China becomes a communist country.

______The last dynasty is defeated.

______Chairman Mao dies.

______Chiang Kai-shek is forced to retreat to Taiwan.

______The Chinese Communist Party is started.

______Famine kills 5 million people.

______The Cultural Revolution begins.

Famous Chinese Folks!

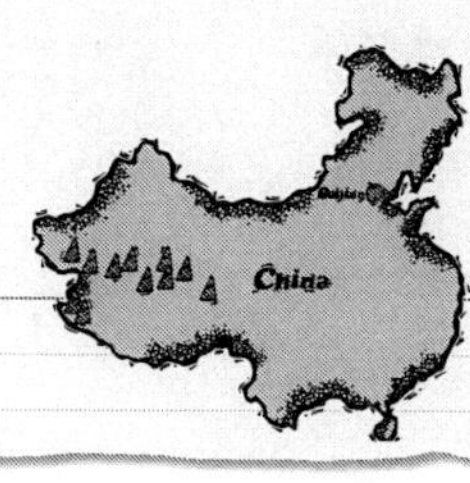

Matching!

Match these famous Chinese folks with their accomplishments

_____1. When I was little, I practiced kung fu every morning with my dad. I graduated from China Drama Academy and went to work as a stuntman. My big break came when I was 21. I was chosen to star in a movie called *New Fist of Fury* in 1976.

_____2. I was born in Venice, Italy in 1254. My father was a merchant who took me with him to Asia when I was 17. Later, I joined the Venetian Army and was captured. While in jail, I met a Frenchman who wrote the stories of my travels.

_____3. By invading southern China, I completed the empire started by my grandfather. I was supreme leader of a Mongol empire that stretched from the Pacific Ocean to the Mediterranean Sea. In 1279, I also became emperor of China.

_____4. More than 2,000 years ago, I developed a plan for a better society. I traveled all over China teaching people about my ideas. My guidelines for a happy and useful life had a great influence on the people of China.

_____5. The art of papermaking was greatly improved with the technology I developed. My paper was light and thin, strong and cheap. Best of all, it could be mass-produced.

_____6. I learned to play chess when I was 17 and in three years became the National Champion of China in 1981. I have won the Chinese Chess Championship seven times.

A. Marco Polo

B. Kublai Khan

C. Confucius

D. Jackie Chan

E. Ye Jiangchuan

F. Cai Lun

Guts and Glory Chinese Style!

Mixed Up!
Match the paragraph to the word that the paragraph describes.

A. Leader of the Chinese Communist Party for more than three decades, he changed the lives of one-fifth of the world's people. He dreamed of a new China and did not tolerate people or views outside the vision. His embalmed body is on display in Tiananmen Square, Beijing.

______

B. In June of 1989, a crowd of students and workers gathered in Tiananmen Square, Beijing, to protest the way their government was run. They wanted more freedom. The government ordered troops and tanks to break up the protest. People around the world were horrified when hundreds of protesters were killed and thousands were arrested.

______

C. It killed 25 million people in Europe between 1347 and 1351. Believed to have started in China, it was spread to Europeans when raiding Mongols catapulted infected corpses into an Italian trading center.

______

D. About 250 people in the world have died from this deadly virus since 2003. The virus is mostly found in birds, but has recently spread to humans. People have little or no immune protection against these viruses because they do not normally infect humans. Many fear that the virus will change and begin to spread from person to person. This could cause a worldwide outbreak of disease.

______

E. It was felt through most of China and as far away as Vietnam and Thailand. Nearly 10,000 people were killed in central China on May 12, 2008. Many of the dead were children buried in the rubble of their schools.

______

BIRD FLU ______

______ **2008 EARTHQUAKE**

BLACK PLAGUE ______

______ **MAN IN FRONT OF TANK**

______ **CHAIRMAN MAO'S BODY ON DISPLAY**

Guarding the Son of Heaven!

In 1974, farmers digging a well in China's Xi'an, Shaanxi province discovered an army of life-size soldiers! These soldiers may have been life-size, but they were never alive. They were all made of clay! The soldiers carried real weapons made of bronze. Some of them rode in beautiful war chariots. The soldiers were arranged in military formation in infantry battle order.

This "Terracotta Army" was created around 221 B.C.E. by the Emperor Qin Shi Huangdi. When Qin Shi Huangdi united the warring states of China, he gave himself the title Emperor, Son of Heaven. The title of emperor was used by all rulers of Imperial China until the 20th century.

Terracotta Army

Qin Shi Huangdi united China by making a standard for weights and measures used in trade. He standardized Chinese writing so the people could understand each other. And he started a huge building campaign—the Great Wall of China.

The emperor also built a huge tomb for himself, guarded by 8,000 clay soldiers. It took more than 700,000 workers to build it! Amazingly, the brightly-painted statues are personal portraits. No two are alike! It is thought that the different faces celebrate the unification of China.

A Personal Portrait!
Get out your crayons. Draw a picture of yourself, your own personal portrait!

Cool Calligraphy!

The Chinese people don't just read words. They look at the way the words are written. Handwriting is considered the "fingerprint" of someone's thoughts!

This attitude toward handwriting came with the invention of paper during the Han Dynasty. The Chinese believed that the written character revealed a person's inner character. Every movement made by a writer could be seen on the paper.

Smooth and bold writing might mean the person is courageous. Sloppy characters could indicate a lazy person. "Calligraphy" means "beautiful writing," and the Chinese consider calligraphy to be the highest art form.

Calligraphy, poetry, and painting are called the "Three Perfections" in China. The Chinese believe that this combination is the height of artistic expression. It is also the sign of an educated person. As a result, more people practice these arts in China than in the West. They often use all three on a single work!

What are you thinking?

Use your imagination to write your name in a way that tells something about your character. Are you bold and adventurous? Shy and timid? How might that look?

China: The Great Wall

The Great Wall of China is one of the most amazing structures built by mankind! It stretches 4,000 miles across extremely rugged terrain! The wall protected China from invading armies.

It took many years to complete the wall and many civilians to get the job done. There are very small sections that have been preserved today. Even more of the wall will continue to disappear in the next 20 years due to erosion. The wall is a popular tourist attraction and is highly recognized in Chinese culture.

The Great Wall of China stretches a total of 4,160 miles!

The Great Wall is the longest man-made structure ever built.

Two to three million Chinese citizens died in the process of building this wall over several centuries.

Although the Great Wall of China is technically not one of the "seven wonders of the world," it was named a UNESCO World Heritage Site in 1987.

Before the use of bricks, the Chinese used earth, stones, and wood.

Create your very own travel pamphlet.
Concentrate on an area that interests you. Perhaps you enjoyed learning about the people. Or maybe it was the monuments that interested you. Fold a piece of paper into three sections. This will give you six areas on which to put information.

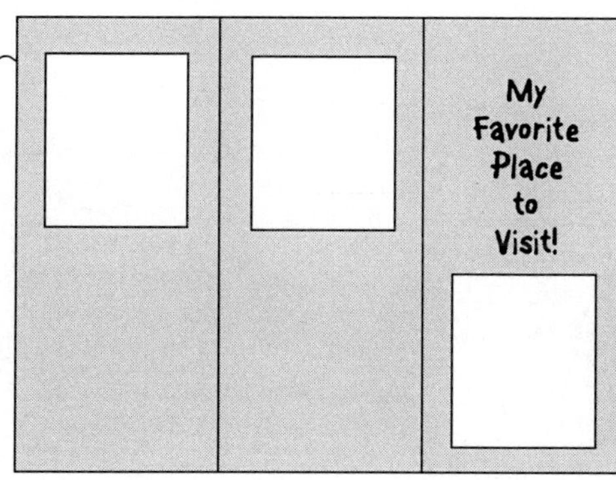

Burp Out Loud!

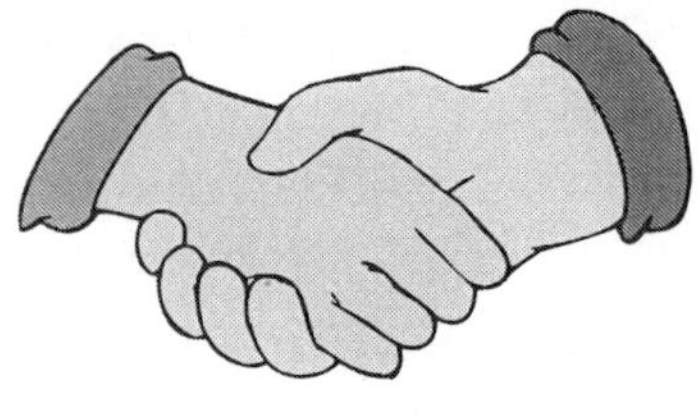

Customs and culture vary widely from country to country. Sometimes they vary in different regions of the same country. Here are customs and cultural differences observed by the Chinese!

- The Chinese often look at the ground when greeting someone. It is considered disrespectful to look into someone's eyes.
- First names and last names are reversed. Fong Ying's given name is Ying and her family name is Fong. You would greet her as Miss Fong.
- Do not use someone's first name until they ask you to do so.
- Flowers are not considered an appropriate gift, since they are associated with funerals.
- Burping and belching during a meal is considered a sign that the food is being enjoyed!
- Never insult, embarrass, or yell at someone in public. This is considered a loss of "face," or honor, and brings shame to the person being insulted.
- The Chinese New Year is one of the most exciting and important events in the country. It celebrates family.
- Snake meat, cat meat, and shark fin are ingredients in some of China's most popular dishes!
- Tapping four fingers down on the table means, "Thank you!"

Create your own!

As we have seen, customs and cultural activities can help define who we are. Think about your family and friends and come up with some new customs for everyone to try.

Kanji? What's a Kanji?

The official language in China is Chinese. They use a different alphabet. Their alphabet is the *Kanji* alphabet.

Match it up!
Below are some common Chinese phrases or words. See if you can match them to the English word.

fei	friend
ai	hair
peng-you	rice
shui	love
mi-fan	swimming pool
qu	day
you-youg	fly
tian	go
you-yong-chi	water
tou-fa	swim

Happy Holidays!

China has several national holidays, including **International Women's Day**, **Labor Day, International Children's Day** (all kids are king for a day!), and the **People's Republic of China's Birthday**.

The most important holiday is the **Chinese New Year**. The New Year usually starts in late January and lasts for 15 days. It is an important time for families. The celebration includes parades, fireworks, and parties.

The last day of the festival is known as the lantern festival. People hang lanterns in temples and carry them in a parade. The highlight of this day is the dragon dance. The bamboo, paper, and silk dragon may be 100 feet long and is carried through the streets by several people who make it look like it's dancing!

Write it down!

Pretend you are visiting China during the Chinese New Year. Write a letter to your best friend. Tell him or her what you have seen. Describe the parades and fireworks. Be as detailed as possible.

China on the Stage and in Museums!

China's deep cultural tradition extends to the arts of health and longevity. It is the birthplace of *Tai Chi*. The National Museum of China is open seven days a week and closes only on the day before Chinese New Year.

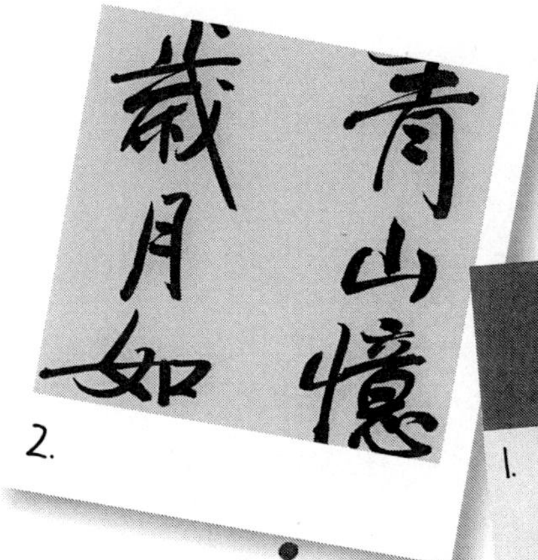

2.

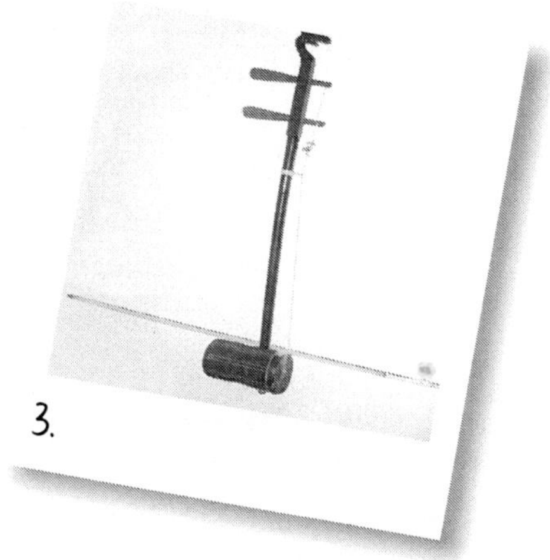

3.

Notes

1. The tradition of China's paper cuts date back to 386-581 C.E. The animals of the Chinese zodiac are this art form's most common theme.
2. The basic technique of Chinese calligraphy has remained unchanged for 2,000 years.
3. The *gao-hu*, a high-pitched Chinese two-stringed fiddle, is a member of the Chinese orchestra.
4. *Tai Chi* was a powerful art of self-defense. Today it is a slow-motion, moving meditative exercise for relaxation and health.
5. Chinese ink paintings like Fan Qi's *Landscapes Painted for Yuweng* have developed continuously for more than 6,000 years.

1.

5.

4.

What's for Dinner?

Chinese food is known for its variety and flavor. Some popular cooking styles include Mandarin, Szechwan, and Cantonese. Rice, potatoes, tofu, noodles, and fish are often used in their dishes. Take a look below and see what you would eat if you visited China.

Dim sum is a kind of Chinese appetizer. Small portions of a variety of foods are served one after the other.

Bok choy is a vegetable with dark green leaves and thick white stems.

Fortune cookies are made from a thin layer of dough that is folded and baked. A written fortune is baked inside the cookie.

Soy sauce is a salty, dark brown sauce made of fermented soybeans. It is used in many Chinese dishes.

Pasta was invented in China, not Italy!

RECIPE

Always ask an adult for help when cooking!

Almond Cookies

INGREDIENTS

1 cup cake flour
3/4 cup powdered sugar
1/4 teaspoon salt
1/2 cup finely ground blanched almonds
6 tablespoons peanut oil
1 egg, well beaten
1 teaspoon almond extract
Whole blanched almonds

mmmmmmmm...this was good!

DIRECTIONS

In a large bowl, sift flour, sugar, salt, and ground almonds together. Add oil and stir. Stir in egg and almond extract. Roll dough to a 1/4-inch thickness and cut into small rounds. Press whole almond into the center of each cookie. Place cookies on a greased cookie sheet. Bake at 375° for 15 minutes. Remove from the oven and place on a cooling rack to cool. Makes 2 dozen cookies.

Martial Arts

Every day as dawn breaks, the streets of China begin to fill with people gathering to perform traditional exercises called taijiqian (t'ai chi ch' uan). Many of the exercises are based on the movements of an animal, such as a tiger, panther, monkey, snake, or crane. These exercises are part of a practice of good health and self-defense known as gongfu. You might know it as kung fu!

Kung fu began long ago when farmers used their tools to fight wild animals. Then it became a method of training soldiers. Wrestling, swords, and spears became part of kung fu training. Testing and competitions in which titles and awards were given made the sport even more popular.

In 1999, martial arts, including kung fu, joined the ranks of Olympic competition. This was a sign of the sport's widespread popularity and appeal!

Figure it out!

Figure out the answers to these questions about martial arts.

1. Matthew has just started to take some lessons in martial arts. He must test twice with each rank after purple belt to move up. Belts are ranks. The ranking order is white, orange, yellow, blue, purple, red, brown, and black. How many times will he test before he can receive his black belt?

   ____

2. Each week students must attend at least three classes in martial arts. At the end of the year, what is the minimum number of classes that students must attend?

   ____

Did you know?
Kung fu is a term used to denote expertise in any endeavor!

Beijing, a City by Many Other Names

For more than 3,000 years, Beijing has been China's capital! This ancient city is China's center of higher learning and culture as well as the seat of government. Over time, the city has changed. Each ruler has had a different idea about how the capital city should look. Glimpses of those visions can still be seen in Beijing today.

The city has also had many names. First, it was Beijing, then Ji, Zhongdu, Dadu, and back to Beijing in 1421. Before 1949, it was known as Peking by the Western world. After 1949, the city became known as Beijing again.

Today, China's capital and second-largest city has a population of about 17 million people! In 2008, it was the site of the Olympic Games.

The name Beijing means "northern capital." The city straddles the divide between Inner and Outer China in the North China Plain. Mountains cover more than half of this capital city.

Word Fun!

In Beijing, modern sites are mixed with ancient. Place the sites in the correct column.

The Great Wall, shopping mall, Forbidden City, Meridian Gate, Imperial Clock Collection, Temple of Heaven, restaurants, Tomb of Mao Zedong, cell phone store

New	Ancient

China Did It First!

Word Fun!

This is fun to do with someone else. Ask a friend for words to substitute for the blanks in the story. Their word substitutions will have a humorous effect when the resulting story is then read aloud.

I want to be the first person to ______________ (ACTION VERB) across ______________ (COUNTRY)! I've been training for this since ______________ (MONTH). I'm in ______________ (ADJECTIVE) shape. My ______________ (ADJECTIVE) adventure will begin on ______________ (FAVORITE HOLIDAY). I won't be hard to miss; I'll be the one wearing a ______________ (COLOR) ______________ (ARTICLE OF CLOTHING) and a pair of matching ______________ (FOOTWEAR). My faithful friends ______________ (FAMOUS ATHLETE) and ______________ (CARTOON CHARACTER) will be there to cheer for me. I'm bringing my ______________ (NOUN) along for good luck. I'm confident I'll be the first!

The Water on the Wheel Goes Round and Round!
Du Shi, a Chinese mechanical engineer, is credited with being the first to use hydraulic power (a water wheel) to power the blast furnace.

Rise and Shine!
The earliest mechanical clock was completed in China in 725 C.E. by I Xing and Liang Lingzan.

Can You See It?
The longest wall in the world is the Great Wall of China. It is 2,150 miles long and took 200 years to build.

No More Writer's Cramp!
Bì Shēng was the inventor of the first known movable type printing system. His invention, made of baked clay, occurred between 1041 and 1048.

Which Way Is South?
The magnetic compass was first invented in China.

Funny, It Doesn't Feel Crowded!
China is the most populated country in the world, with more than 1.3 billion people.

Hitting the Bullseye!
Gunpowder was first invented in China and was used to create an early form of fireworks.

Wolong Panda Reserve

High in the mountains of China's Sichuan Province is one of the last protected homes of the giant panda. The Wolong Panda Preserve is one way the Chinese government is fighting to protect these lovable creatures whose habitat is quickly disappearing! By studying the pandas and their natural environment, scientists hope to learn how to help them survive.

The preserve includes the most successful breeding center in the world for giant pandas. Each year, panda babies are born there. The birth of a baby panda is always a celebration since these gentle animals often have difficulty reproducing in the wild.

The red panda, snow leopard, takin, Asiatic black bear, and golden snub-nose monkey also find protection in the forests and ice-covered mountains of the preserve. More than 6,000 species of plants and animals can be found on the 494,200 acres set aside in 1963!

Wolong means "sleeping dragon." It describes the mountain peaks running through the nature reserve and the surrounding area.

Word Fun!

Write 5 questions that might need to be answered in order to help an endangered animal survive.

Example: What food does it eat?

1. ______________________________?
2. ______________________________?
3. ______________________________?
4. ______________________________?
5. ______________________________?

The Forbidden City

"The purple city where one cannot enter." That's the English translation of Tzu Chin Ch'eng, the city of palaces in the center of China's capital, Beijing! This city of palaces became known as the "Forbidden City." Building this magnificent inner city took more than 14 years and millions of workers.

Yung Le, the third Ming emperor, built the city as a monument to his rule. He believed the city linked him to the divine forces of the world. According to legend, his tutor had a dream in which the structure and color of the city was revealed. In the dream, the Lord of Heaven lives in a purple constellation formed by 15 heavenly bodies turning around the North Star. The color purple was a symbol of joy and happiness. Only the emperor could use it. Keeping harmony between humans and the natural world was the emperor's job.

The five elemental colors were included in the design of the city—white terraces, black courtyards, red columns, yellow roofs, and blue sky reflected in the moat. The Forbidden City was home to 24 emperors who ruled China for more than 500 years. It was the political center of China until 1912 when the last emperor was defeated.

The Forbidden City

Revealing Answer!

Follow the instructions to reveal where the Forbidden City is located.

1. Cross off the first and last letters.
2. Cross off any letter "O."
3. Cross off the letter that represents the Roman numeral 10.
4. Cross off the second "E" from the left.
5. Cross off the tenth letter from the right.
6. Cross off the third and last letters of the alphabet.

ABOCEXIZQEOJIXNGOM

____

The Cultural Revolution

The communist ruler of China, Chairman Mao Zedong, worried that he was losing power. But he was not about to give up! Anyone who disagreed with Chairman Mao was beaten, imprisoned, or sent away to work on communes. Children were told to turn in their parents for suspected wrongs. The Red Guard searched homes to destroy any evidence of other opinions. No one was above suspicion!

Mao Zedong

Chairman Mao declared a Great Cultural Revolution. He formed an army called the Red Guard to help him erase all evidence of China's past. Ancient buildings and priceless art were destroyed. Hundreds of thousands of government officials and professionals were accused of holding the wrong view. Many of China's smartest people were sent away.

Mao's Cultural Revolution came to an end in 1969. The ruthless Red Guard was defeated. When Mao died in 1976, his wife and three Communist Party officials tried to take over the government. Many people blamed them for Mao's Cultural Revolution. They were arrested and jailed.

Cross it off!

Starting with the first letter, cross off every other letter to reveal the name of the group who tried to take over the Chinese government after the death of Mao.

XTDHREQGPALNKGMOBFVFCOEUYR

____

Hanging Monastery

Have you ever seen a building hanging from a cliff? You can—in China!

At the foot of Mt. Hengshan, a monastery hangs on the west cliff of Jinxia Gorge. More than 150 feet from the ground, it is an architectural wonder! Construction experts from countries around the world come to study the framework.

The Hanging Monastery was built in 491 and has survived more than 1,400 years. The location was chosen for two reasons. At 150 feet off the ground, the monastery is protected from flooding. The mountain shelters it from rain and snow. Most importantly, the builders followed a principle in Taoism: no noises! Not even the sound of dogs barking or roosters crowing can be heard from so high off the ground.

Hanging Monastery

Inside the monastery, China's three traditional belief systems are represented. Only here, Buddhist, Taoist, and Confucian sculptures sit side-by-side.

Figure it out!

The five sacred Taoist mountains are associated with the five cardinal directions. For the Chinese, the center was included as a direction. Fill in the blanks and discover the direction of each mountain.

Leading Peaceful Mountain ___ A ___ ___

Balancing Mountain ___ O ___ ___ ___

Splendid Mountain ___ E ___ ___

Permanent Mountain ___ ___ R ___ ___

Lofty Mountain ___ E ___ ___ ___ ___ ___

Did you know?
The Hengshan Mountains are one of China's five sacred mountain ranges. Mountains were thought to be sacred because they were seen as pillars separating heaven and earth.

Silk Cheongsam
(chung som)

The *Cheongsam* is a long, decorated dress which has become a symbol of Chinese identity. Worn by both men and women, the close-fitting gown with slits on the side is also called a *Qipao* (chee pow). It came from the Manchus in the early 17th century.

Legend tells of a smart, young fisherwoman who lived by Jingbo Lake. The loose dress that she wore made it hard to fish. She decided to make a dress that was better suited for work. She made a long, buttoned dress with slits. She could tuck in the front of her dress, making it better suited for fishing.

The emperor had a dream one night. In his dream, his father told him that a beautiful fisherwoman who lived by the lake would become his queen. When he awoke, he sent his men to the lake to find her. She became the queen and brought her *Cheongsam* with her. Soon all the women of Manchu would wear the *Cheongsam*!

Figure it out!

A famous Chinese fashion designer needs your help to get dressed for her tour of China! Below are some clothing styles you might see in China today. Choose which outfit she'll wear. Color the clothing, and draw a line from the piece of clothing to her or cut the clothing out and dress her up.

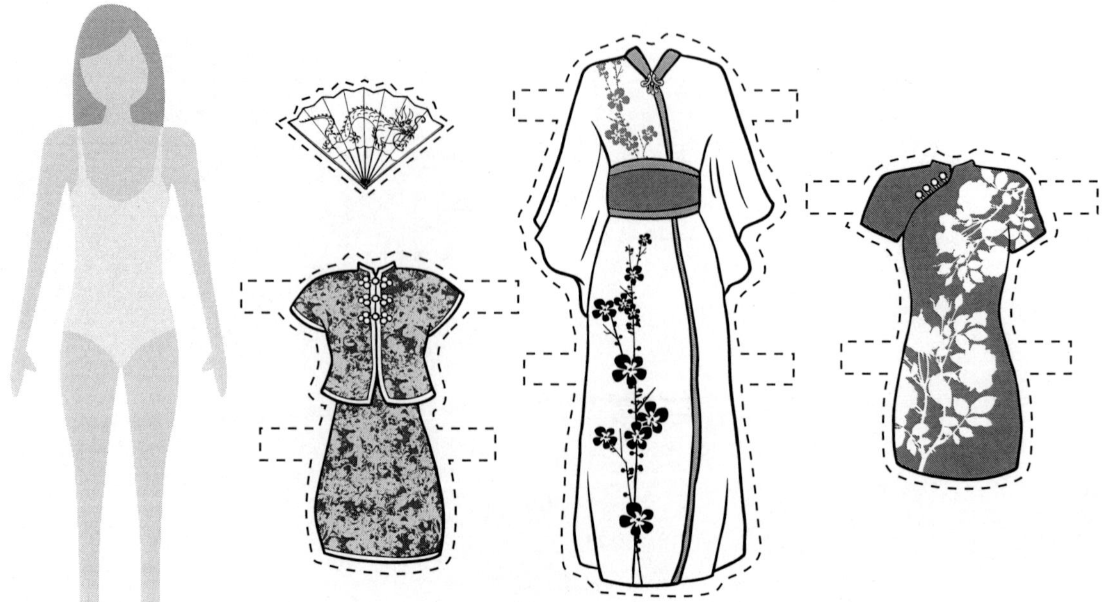

Assorted Architecture!

Figure it out!
Use the following clues to figure out the name of this famous building in Beijing, China.

- The grandest and most holy of Beijing Imperial temples.
- The emperor came here every winter solstice to pray for a good harvest.
- The ceremony was considered so sacred that commoners had to bolt their windows and remain in silence indoors throughout the event.
- Animal sacrifices were performed before the Throne of Heaven at the Round Altar.
- The temple complex was forbidden to everyone but the emperor and his court.
- Considered to be the middle of Middle Kingdom and the very center of the earth.

As They Say in China...

Here are a few Chinese words you may already know. Why? Because we use them as "English" words all the time!

catsup/ketchup: a condiment made from tomatoes
chop-chop: quickly, without delay
chopstick: slender wooden eating utensil; looks like a stick
chop suey: miscellaneous bits, a dish prepared from vegetables, meat or fish, and rice
chow: food; also spinoff words such as chow time, chow line, chowhound
chow chow: a type of dog
chow mein: a stew of shredded meat, mushrooms, vegetables, and noodles
cumshaw: a present
dim sum: variety of traditional Chinese food served in small portions
gob: sailor
honcho: leader of a group
kowtow: to kneel and touch the forehead to the ground to show respect
kumquat: small yellow orange citrus fruit used chiefly for preserves
shanghai: kidnap someone to do a job
silk: a shimmering cloth made from cocoons of the silkworm
soy: sauce made from fermenting soybeans in brine
tai pan: a leading business entrepreneur; person who starts businesses
typhoon: a great windstorm, hurricane

Further Resources

U.S. Embassy in China
Xiu Shui Bei Jie 3, 100600
Phone: (86-10) 6532-3831

United Nations
2 United Nations Plaza
New York, NY 10017

China National Tourist Office, New York
370 Lexington Ave. #912
New York, NY 10017 USA
Phone: (212) 760-8218
Fax: (212) 760-809
ny@cnto.org

Beijing Tourism Administration
Webmaster_en@bjta.gov.cn

Interesting Websites

http://www.greatwall-of-china.com/

http://www.yangtzeriver.org/

http://www.chinavista.com/

http:// www.ebeijing.gov.cn

Answer Key

Page 7
1. flag 2. symbol 3. anthem 4. official
5. population 6. Middle Kingdom

Page 8
1. a 2. c

Page 9

Page 10
5, 1, 7, 4, 2, 3, 6

Page 11
1. D 2. A 3. B 4. C 5. F 6. E

Page 12
Bird Flu – D; 2008 Earthquake – E;
Black Plague – C; Man in front of tank – B;
Chairman Mao's body on display – A

Page 17

fei	fly
ai	love
peng-you	friend
shui	water
mi-fan	rice
qu	go
you-youg	swim
you-yong-chi	swimming pool
tian	day
tou-fa	hair

Page 21
1. 6 times
2. 156 classes

Page 22
New: shopping mall, restaurants, Tomb of Mao, Imperial Clock collection

Ancient: Great Wall, Forbidden City, Temple of Heaven, Meridian Gate

Page 25
Beijing

Page 26
The Gang of Four

Page 27
1. east 2. south 3. west 4. north 5. central

Page 29
Temple of Heaven